Contents

3

Introduction.

Farmstead cheeses are most often made on family farms in small batches and is often sold at local farmers' markets. While Europe has long had a very strong tradition of farmstead cheese-making, it is only in the last decades of the 20th century that farmstead cheese-making began to return to prominence in North America. In the United States, the top states for farmstead cheesmaking include Vermont, California, and Wisconsin, although farmstead cheese is growing rapidly in other states, like Georgia, as well. North Carolina is another state that has recently gained accolades for its farmstead cheeses, even creating the WNC Cheese Trail.

In Europe these cheeses are more commonly known as farmhouse cheeses and there are many different varieties available, especially from Ireland and Germany. The small scale of production allows for unique sales points such as cheese from cows raised on non-genetically modified organisms (GMOs)-containing feed

Farmstead cheese, less commonly known as farmhouse cheese, is produced from the milk collected on the same farm where the cheese is produced. Unlike artisan cheese, which may also include milk purchased and transported from off-farm sources, farmstead cheese makers only use milk from animals they raise.According to the American Cheese Society, "milk used in the production of farmstead cheeses may not be obtained from any outside source".As a result, the cheeses produced often have unique flavors owing to the farm's local terroir. Most farmstead cheese is produced from cow, goat or sheep milk, although some farmstead cheeses are produced from water buffalo milk (mainly Buffalo mozzarella).

Procedures For Processing Milk For Farm Stead Cheese.

These Farmstead cheeses were prone to quite a range of interpretations:

- They tended to be made in all different sizes and weights.
- Some were colored to a medium or even bright orange, others had no color added.
- They could range in moisture levels and potential for aging in the cool room or cellar.
- They could be heavily pressed with a close tight texture, or lightly pressed with some openness in the body.

- Some were waxed and some were wrapped and pressed with a cloth bandage.

- Some were placed in the sun to pull the moisture out, others went directly to aging

- So, as you can see here, the cheese could be whatever the maker wanted. However, they all seemed to know how to ripen the milk and curds properly, and to dry the curds enough before pressing to avoid spoilage.

We do suggest for the initial trial to stay close to the guidelines and take lots of notes, and then venture off in future cheese making sessions, after you have tasted the cheese you have aged

How To Get Started

Acidify & Heat Milk

Begin by heating the milk to 88°F (32°C). You do this by placing the milk in a pot or sink of very warm water. If you do this in a pot on the stove, make sure you heat the milk slowly and stir it well as it heats.

If you opt to use the annatto for coloring your cheese, the final color is rather subjective, so anywhere from 2-8 ml for this volume of milk should give you a pale gold to deep red orange. This can be added as you are heating the milk, being sure to stir it well.

All pasturized and cold stored milk should have 1/4-1/2 tsp calcium chloride added to replace the usable calcium that has been lost. This can be added as you are heating the milk, being sure to stir it well. Once the milk is at 88°F, the culture can be added.

Note: I sometimes find that the entire pack can be a bit much for the 2 gallons, so try adding only 3/4 of the pack if you are having problems with the cheese being sour in flavor and crumbly.

To prevent the powder from caking and sinking in clumps, sprinkle the powder over the surface of the milk and then allow about 2 minutes for the powder to re-hydrate before stirring it in. The milk then needs to be kept at 88F for about 60 minutes.

Add about 1/2 tsp or 2.5ml of single strength liquid rennet. The milk now needs to set still for 30 minutes while the culture works and the rennet coagulates the curd.

The milk will start to thicken at about 8-10 minutes. In the Ehle book, Mrs. Kirby talks about an age old trick to see this thickening; a piece of clean toothpick is dropped on the surface, and when this becomes dead still, the milk is beginning it's final stage of coagulation. Multiplying this by 3.5 should give you the 30 minute coagulation you need for this cheese.

The thermal mass of this milk should keep it warm during this period. It is OK if the temperature drops a few degrees during this time.

Cut Curd & Release Whey

When the coagulation is complete, it is time to cut the curds and release the whey. You can easily see the quality of your coagulation by inserting the flat of a knife blade at an angle into the curd and then lifting straight up. If the edges are clean breaks and the whey pools neither too clear nor too cloudy in the gap, you have a good curd for cutting.

The curd now needs to be cut into 3/8 to 5/8 inch pieces, using a knife to make the vertical cuts and a spoon or ladle for the horizontal cuts. The curd may not be even in size, but do the best you can in cutting. After the cutting, the curd needs to be stirred slowly but steadily at the original temperature for about 5-10 minutes. This will cause some whey to be released, allowing the curds to move freely. The surface will begin to firm up slightly as well.

As the curds release whey, the surface firms up. The large curd piece (being held in the photo above) shows a skin forming and drying off the exterior. However, when the curd is broken open, it is very soft, wet and tender inside. This is why we take a very long time to dry out the curd in the next step. If the skin becomes too firm and thick, as in heating too quickly or stirring too fast, it will be difficult to dry out the inside of the curd. This will result in a wet curd going into the mold and problems in aging.

Now it is time to begin drying out the curds. This will be done by increasing the heat slowly to 102°F. The heat needs to be increased slowly at about 2-3°F every 5 minutes at the beginning. The total cooking time will be 30-45 minutes.

Once the curds are at temperature, they should be stirred in the whey just enough to keep them separated and moving. The bacteria are still developing the needed acidity and the curds will be drying out during this period.

This should be done for another 1-1.5 hrs depending on the dryness of the cheese desired. During this stirring time, at 15 minutes intervals, allow the curds to settle for a few minutes but do not allow the curds to mat together, then remove about a pint or two of whey before stirring again.

Stirring these curds in the whey like this will give them access to the lactose rich whey for further acid development, as well as allow for easier movement of the curds. The final curds should be cooked well through and should be examined to make sure that enough moisture has been removed. A broken curd should be firm throughout and the curds should have a moderate resistance when pressed between the fingers.

When this point is reached, the curds can be allowed to settle under the whey

Remove Whey & Salt Curds

The dry curds can now be transferred to a colander lined with butter muslin. They should be allowed to drain for 30 minutes and a gentle stirring will make sure that the whey drains off.

At the point of final whey drainage, the curd will have reached its final moisture and acid development and should be salted immediately to stop the action of the bacteria. About 2% salt should be added according to final curd weight (approx 2 lbs). This should be about .62 oz or about 3 tsp of salt. Add this in two doses and allow it to dissolve between doses, before moving to filling the molds.

Form the Curds

Once the curds are drained and salted, they are ready for the mold. Prepare the mold and cloth by sanitizing, then line the mold with the cloth and transfer the curds using a good hand pressure to pack the curds in tight.

For pressing I use our Hard Cheese Press, but it is possible to make a simple lever press (sometimes known as a dutch press). The illustration above is a simple schematic from the 1934 brochure Making American Cheese on the Farm, it's a good guide to follow.

Press the Curds

Now, for pressing, we should begin very light and slowly increase the press weight to a moderate level:

- 60 minutes at 10 lbs
- 3 hours at 25 lbs
- 18 hours at 50 lbs turning once midway and returning to press

The rate of whey running off is initially a thin stream, tapering to steady drops of whey being released. This is a good rate of whey removal during pressing and will slow even more as the residual free moisture is released. You should see whey weeping from the form very slowly. When this stops, you can increase the weight slightly. The cheese should be removed from the press, unwrapped, turned, re-wrapped, and put back to the press at the above intervals to assure an even consolidation. At each turn you will notice the cheese has formed a smoother surface and rests lower in the mold.

The cheese should begin coming together after the first or second press cycle but you may still notice some gaps and holes between the curds By the end of the third cycle (50 lbs) it should be well consolidated as shown above.

If you still see some openings in the surface, due to a dry curd, then increase the press weight to 75 lbs and press until the cheese forms a tight surface with no openings:

Final Preparation & Aging

The cheese should be allowed to surface dry for about 1-5 days (this will depend on room conditions). Flip the cheese twice a day and watch for the surface to darken a bit.

The cheese can then be placed into your aging space at 52-56°F and 80-85% moisture. The cheese can now be aged for 4-6 weeks and it will ready for your table.

Farm Stead Cheese Recipes

CamBlu is a rather modern style of cheese. This recipe is a great opportunity to experience making a hybrid cheese by combining two separate styes, Camembert with a mushroomy rind and soft paste with the added flavor from a mild Blue Cheese inside. The Blue simply melts into the creamy Camembert when this cheese is ripe.

- Yield: 3 Pounds
- Aging: Time Under 2 Months

Ingredients:

- 2 Gallons of Milk (Not UltraPasteurized)
- 8-12 oz Heavy Cream
- 1 Packet C21 Buttermilk Culture or 1/4 tsp MM100 or C11 Flora Danica
- 1/64 tsp Penicillium Roqueforti
- 1/8 tsp Penicillium Candidum
- 1/32 tsp Geotrichum Candidum
- 1/4 tsp (1.25ml) Single Strength Liquid Rennet
- Cheese Salt
- Calcium Chloride (for pasteurized milk)

Equipment:

- Good Thermometer

- Knife to Cut Curds

- Spoon or ladle to Stir Curds

- 3-4 Camembert Cheese Molds

- Draining Mats

Instructions:

- Acidify & Heat Milk

Begin by heating the milk to 90°F (32°C). You do this by placing the milk in a pot or sink of very warm water. If you do this in a pot on the stove, make sure you heat the milk slowly and stir it well as it heats.

Once the milk is at 90°F, the acidifying culture only should be added. To prevent the powder from caking and sinking in clumps, sprinkle the powder over the surface of the milk and then allow about 2 minutes for the powder to re-hydrate before stirring it in. Do not add any of the Blue or White ripening molds at this time.

Allow the culture added milk to ripen for 30 minutes while keeping warm. This is a shorter than normal ripening time because there will be a very long coagulation time for the bacteria to do it's work converting lactose to lactic acid. This will allow the bacteria to prepare for their work ahead.

- Coagulate with Rennet

After the short 30 minute ripening, add about 1/4 tsp (1.25ml) of single strength liquid rennet.

The milk now needs to sit quiet for 90 minutes. This small amount of rennet was added to begin the initial coagulation in a short period of time (15-20 min.) but allow the final firming of the curd to continue for a much longer period of time (90 minutes or more from rennet addition). This will result in a curd that tends to hold the moisture and fat better due to the stronger protein matrix.

You will notice the milk beginning to thicken slightly in about 18 minutes, but continue to allow to set for the full time. The thermal mass of this milk should keep it warm during this period. It is OK if the temperature drops a few degrees during this time. The long coagulation time here is to loosely hold more of the water in the curd and to allow a moister curd to be transferred to the molds.

While waiting for the coagulation, the forms, draining mats, and boards need to be sanitized and prepared for the curd transfer. I do this here by submerging in 145°F water for several minutes.

- Cut Curd & Release Whey

A departure from traditional Camembert or Brie will be noted once the curd has formed. In the traditional cheese, little to no cutting was needed, but to preserve some air space in the interior, a typical blue production step is needed here.

The curds should be cut to about 3/4 inch cubes and then Very Gently And Slowly stirred. This will be focused on drying the exterior of the curd while still preserving the high moisture internally. This gentle curd movement should continue at 90F for about 20-30 minutes and I emphasize the SLOW and Gentle. The actual stir time will depend upon you and the milk you are using. It may take a few batches to get it right so observe what is happening and take lots of notes.

Essentially, you are looking to preserve as much moisture inside the curds for the final cheese and at the same time hardening the curd exterior enough so that they leave a bit of air space (nooks and crannies so to speak) when molded. The blue needs air to do it's magic.

- Begin Forming Cheese

Once the curds have developed the proper character, it is time to move them to the molds for draining and further acid development. The curds should now have a drier exterior with a slight skin formed while still retaining lots of moisture inside. When placed in the molds, they should not be expected to consolidate as well as the traditional Camembert or Brie.

Normally, I would use 4 of the Camembert molds for this cheese but since we have left more whey behind during the stirring and hardening, I find that 3 molds will work best here. Actually I find it provides a taller cheese which I like better for this style. The forms should have been sanitized and ready on the draining table at this point.

Begin by settling the curds and removing about 20% of the whey before taking the first of the curds to the molds. It is best to use a slotted spoon or ladle for the transfer because excess whey will carry off the blue mold you will be adding. Transfer about 1/2-3/4 inches of curd to each form making sure the base is covered.

- Add Blue Mold, Finish Forming

Taking just a pinch (~1/64 tsp) of the Penicillium.roqueforti, carefully sprinkle as evenly as possible across the surface, trying to keep in from the edges (avoids blue on the exterior of the cheese).

Transfer another 1/2-3/4 inches of curd to the mold. Follow this with the same blue addition as in step 2. Continue these layers until you have just enough curd for a final top layer of curd.

Add the final 1/2-3/4 inch layer of curd to encapsulate the blue inside the cheese.

- Draining the Whey

The next stage is to allow the whey to drain off as the acid production continues. During this, the forms need to be turned on a regular basis. The way to do this is to place another draining mat and board on top of the form then Carefully and quickly flip it over. This is best done before the curd settles too far into the mold. The curd mass should drop evenly to the new draining surface with no breakage. This initial turn will set a nice smooth surface for the final cheese.

The turning of the cheese needs to be done several times during the draining process to assure an even drainage of the curd.

By the next morning, the cheese should have drained to about 1/2-1/3 of its original height and the final acid level should be correct. I do try to keep the curds warm (68-72°F) during this period to assure the proper whey drainage. I use an insulated sink here with an insulated pad and board to keep the temperatures good for acid development and drainage (70-75°F). A pan or bottles of warm water would also be good for keeping the temperatures during cooler weather. A simple insulated cooler would also work for this.

Note the open surface in the photos above. This will run through the cheese body and provide plenty of air space for the blue to grow.

- Salting

At this point, I remove the form and then add the first dose of salt to the surface of each cheese. 1/2 tsp of a medium crystal cheese salt is added and then evenly spread over the surface. This can then be lightly spread to the outside edge as well. There will be less salt on the edge but the next application will also be applied to the edge and that will even out the distribution. When finished, place back in forms with salt side up and leave until the salt dissolves in the cheese moisture and eventually into the cheese. In about 4-6 hours, flip the cheese and repeat on the other side.

- Drying & Aging

Drying the cheese: The next morning (day 3) the mold can be removed and the cheese placed on a dry surface to begin the drying phase. This should continue until all surface moisture is done. In humid areas a small fan may be needed. This is best done in a room of 58-65°F and 60-75% moisture. Turning several times during the drying will also help.

Note:

If the cheese is moved to the aging area before the proper draining/drying phase is complete, excessive moisture will cause defects such as mucor or blue mold and increased protein breakdown at the surface resulting in runny cheese during aging.

The aging space: Once the cheese surface is dried (about 1-2 days after draining has completed), it is time to move to the aging area. This should be maintained at 92-95% humidity and 52-56°F. The cheese should be turned once or twice daily at this phase. Failure to do this may result in excess mold growth growing into the mats and tearing the surface on removal.

To maintain this high level of humidity, I use plastic trays with covers and bamboo draining mats to provide air circulation under the cheese.

- Aeration for Blue Mold

About 1-2 days after moving cheese to the aging area is the the time to pay attention to the ripening molds. The first thing we will do is make about 20-25 holes in the surface of the cheese, going in at least mid way or further. I use a 1/8 inch stainless steel probe that has been flamed and cooled to eliminate any free bacteria riders. The blue is already in the cheese body and just needs air to do its work now. Make sure you do both sides.

- Inoculation of While Mold

As mentioned previously, if these molds had been added to the milk or sprayed on earlier in the process, their growth would soon spread to the holes and grow over these to block the air needed by the blue.

About 1-2 days after the cheese has been aerated, it is time to spray the white molds onto the surface. A very fine aerosol spray bottle is needed for this. Mix about 1/4 tsp salt into 4 oz. of water and add 1/8 tsp of Penicillium.candidum and 1/32 tsp of Geotrichum into this and allow it to rehydrate overnight. The next morning you can spray lightly onto the surface of the cheese, taking care not to get the surface too wet. Allow the surface to dry slightly then return to the aging space

- Ripening

The cheese is now ready to ripen. Return the cheese to its ripening area and turn it at least once a day. I have seen the candidum grow aggressively enough that I needed to turn twice daily. In about 7-10 more days, the white surface should have developed to a full cover. At this point, it should be placed in an area of 42-46°F but higher humidity. This will slow the ripening and allow the enzymes being produced by the molds to do their work.

If you find that the geotrichum/candidum is growing over the aeration holes for the blue, you may find that you need to punch the surface again to aid the blue growth. The blue mold will be ripening from the center out, whereas the white molds will be working from the outer surface in.

You should be able to determine the ripening progress by feeling the developing softness of the cheese. This final ripening should be in 30-45 days but it is best to monitor your cheese as it progresses.

Gorgonzola Dolce Cheese Making Recipe

Gorgonzola Dolce 'The Sweet One' in Italy this is sometimes known as Cremifacato or Dolcelatte. Traditionally made from cows milk, it has a wonderful flavor that is mild, creamy and sweet. This is a younger version of an aged Gorgonzola and is most loved for the soft, spreadable texture.

- Yield: 2 Pounds
- Aging Time: Under 3 Months

Ingredients:

- 2 Gallons of Milk (Not Ultra Pasteurized)

- 1 Packet Buttermilk Culture

- 2.5 oz Prepared Bulgarian Yogurt

- 1/16 tsp Penicillium Roqueforti

- 1/2 tsp Liquid Single Strength Animal Rennet (1/4 tsp for raw milk)

- Salt

- 1/2 tsp Calcium Chloride (for Pasteurized Milk)

Equipment:

- Good Thermometer

- Measuring Spoons

- Curd Knife

- Skimmer to Stir Curds

- Cheesecloth

- Small Hard Cheese Mold

Instructions:

- Acidify & Heat Milk

Add blue mold to a small amount of milk to rehydrate about 1/2 hour before adding it to the full batch of milk. This allows it to acclimate and incorporate well.

Begin by heating the milk to 90F (32C). You do this by placing the pot of milk in a sink of very warm water. If you do this with a pot on the stove make sure you heat the milk slowly and stir it well as it heats.

 Once the milk is at 90F the cultures and re-hydrated mold can be added. To prevent the powder from caking and sinking in clumps sprinkle the powder over the surface of the milk and then allow about 2 minutes for the powder to re-hydrate before stirring it in. Stir the milk well then stop stirring and allow the bacteria to work for 60 minutes while keeping at 90F (If the cream tends to rise it is OK to stir it back in briefly).

- Coagulate with Rennet

Next add the single strength liquid rennet. The milk now needs to sit quiet for 30 minutes while the culture works and the rennet coagulates the curd . Keep the developing curd at 90F during this time.

- Cut & Stir Curds

Once the curd has formed well it can be cut. Begin with vertical cuts about 1" apart forming a checkerboard pattern on the surface. Then, using the spoon, break the resulting long strips by cutting crosswise in the vat but being very gentle. When finished, stir the curds gently for 5 minutes and then allow the curds to rest for 15 minutes with only a brief gentle stir every 3-5 mines to keep them separated.

At the end of this rest, remove about 1.5-2 quarts of whey from the pot. Again, stir the curds gently for 5 minutes and then allow the curds to rest for 15 minutes with only a brief gentle stir every 3-5 minutes to keep them separated.

This stirring and whey removal will harden the outside of the curds to keep them from matting in the mold. This provides the openings for mold development in the aging cheese. It is important to keep the curds at 90F during all of this.

- Drain Curds

During the resting period, sanitize a colander and butter muslin for the final curd draining. The moist curds can now be transferred to the colander lined with butter muslin. They should be allowed to drain for several minutes and a gentle stirring will make sure that the whey drains off. It is essential to be gentle with these curds, since they are very soft, and not break them. You can assist the drainage by pulling up on the edges of the cloth and gently separating the curds.

Counter to what is done in consolidating curds well for other cheeses, the goal here is to keep the curds separate and allow the surfaces to harden somewhat. This will keep them separated when placed in the molds and preserve the open spaces inside the cheese for the blue to grow.

- Mold Curds

The mold should be sanitized along with 2 of the draining mats. A rigid plate or board placed underneath will also help in turning this cheese. Prepare the mold by laying down a draining mat with the mold placed on top. No cheesecloth needs to be used with this. The curds can now be placed in the molds. They can be packed in more tightly around the edge to make a better surface for the cheese but the center should be quite loose to assure the proper openings for mold growth.

It is quite important to keep the curds warm for the next several hours while the cultures continue to produce acid. I do this by placing the draining curds in a warm draining table with pans of hot water and an insulated cover and board to keep it all warm. You can easily do this by using a large insulated cooler with warm bottles of water. The target temp is 80-90F for the next 4-6 hours.

There is no weight used on this cheese but the mold should be turned 5 minutes after it has been filled to allow the weight of the cheese to form a smooth surface. The cheese should then be turned several more times during the first hour and then at least 1 time each hour for the next 4 hours.

By the next morning the cheese should be well consolidate but you may see some rough surfaces or openings. Do not be concerned by this.

- Salting

We prefer to dry salt this cheese because of the open nature of the cheese body. Normally using about 2-2.5% of the cheese weight in salt for this. For this cheese you will need 1 oz. of a medium coarse cheese salt. This will be about 4 tsp. of our cheese salt but it is better to measure by weight because different salts have different weight/volume ratios.

For dry salting, use 1/4 of the salt to begin with and apply to the top surface only, then spread it evenly with your hand and pat the salt onto the sides as you go. Allow this to dissolve and soak into the cheese. I generally take the cheese out of the mold for salting and then replace it in the mold for the salt to be absorbed.

The next morning turn the cheese and apply the salt as you did previously. Repeat this for the next 2 days as well.

- Aging

The cheese is now ready for aging at 52-54F and 93-95% moisture. If the rind becomes dry, increase the moisture and if the surface becomes excessively wet, decrease moisture.

Allow the cheese to age like this for 7-10 days. Then using a sanitized #2 knitting needle, pierce the cheese with holes about every 3/4 to 1 inch.

The cheese should now be ready for its final aging and will be ready for the table in about 90 days.

Dry Jack Cheese Recipe

Dry Jack Cheese is made with a longer cook and stir time to dry out the curds, then it is pressed in a cloth without cheese molds. Once formed, a spicy surface rub with cocoa, pepper, coffee, and oil is applied to the surface while aging. This process creates a spectacular presentation and a yummy cheese.

- Yield: 6 Pounds
- Aging Time: 6+ Months

Ingredients:

- 6 Gallons of Milk (Not Ultra-Pasteurized)
- 1/4 tsp MA4002 Culture - Can Substitute 1 Packet C101 Mesophilic Culture if Making 2-3 lb Batch
- 3 ml (just over 1/2 tsp) Single Strength Liquid Rennet

- 2.5 oz Salt

- Calcium Chloride for Pasteurized Milk

- 1 tsp Espresso Beans

- 2 tbs Cocoa Nibs

- 1.5 tsp Black Pepper

- 3-3.5 tbs Olive Oil

Equipment:

- Large Stainless Steel Pot

- Good Thermometer

- Knife to Cut Curds

- Spoon or ladle to Stir Curds

- Large Colander

- Butter Muslin

- Draining Mats

- 2-3 Flat Boards for Pressing (wood or plastic is fine)

- 25 lb & 50 lb Weight for Pressing

Instructions:

- This recipe might not be for the start-up cheese maker, but anyone that has made a few hard cheeses is perhaps ready to take it on.

- I have chosen to do a 6 gallon recipe because using a larger mass for forming in the cloth making the final cheese a much more spectacular presentation (and the larger surface makes it easier to balance my final press free weight).

- Of Coarse the recipe can be scaled down proportionately for a 2 gallon batch and the cheese can be done in a small mold with cloth. The smaller cheese does not lend itself to forming into a ball in the cloth so does not have the organic character of using just the natural cloth to form it but will work just fine.

For making a 2 gallon batch Use:

- 2 Gallons of Whole Milk
- 1 Packet C101 Mesophilic Culture

- 1 ml (just under 1/4 tsp) Single Strength Liquid Rennet

The rest of the recipe will be the same as detailed below EXCEPT that the weight will be reduced to:

- 8 lbs (about 1 gallon of water) for 2 hrs and
- 16 lbs for the overnight pressing

Instructions:

- Acidify & Heat Milk

Begin by heating the milk to 90-92°F (32-33°C). You do this by placing the milk in a pot or sink of very warm water. If you do this in a pot on the stove make sure you heat the milk slowly and stir it well as it heats.

Once the milk is at the correct temperature, the culture can be added. To prevent the powder from caking and sinking in clumps, sprinkle the powder over the surface of the milk and then allow about 2 minutes for the powder to re-hydrate before stirring it in.

Allow this milk to ripen for about 45 minutes, stirring occasionally to keep the cream from rising.

- Coagulate with Rennet

Now add about 3 ml or a bit more than 1/2 tsp of single strength liquid rennet. The milk now needs to sit still for 40 minutes while the culture works and the rennet coagulates the curd. The thermal mass of the milk should keep it warm during this period. It is OK if the temp drops a few degrees during this time.

You should notice the milk beginning to thicken at about 16 minutes, but allow it to harden the full time or until you get a firm curd. If the curd is not firm enough to cut at the end of the 40 minutes, allow it to sit longer until a clean break shows in the curd when tested. If it takes longer than 50 minutes you should increase the rennet proportionately the next time you make this cheese. If the milk begins to thicken sooner than the 16 minutes, use less rennet in the next batch.

- Cut Curds & Release Whey

Once the firm curd has formed, it is time to cut the curd and release the whey. The smaller you cut, the drier the final cheese and the longer it can be aged for more complex flavors. Here I usually begin my cut (pre-cut) with a large cross cut of the surface as shown below, then wait 5 minutes for the whey to rise before continuing. I then use a large whisk with expanded wires to cut the cheese into smaller pieces. I generally work to a 1/2-3/8" cut size in the initial curd.

- Cook Curds & Remove Whey

Now it is time to begin drying out the curds. This will be done by increasing the heat slowly to 102°F (39°C). The heat needs to be increased slowly, about 1-2F every 5 minutes. The total cooking time will be 45 minutes.

The final curds should be cooked well through and should be examined to make sure that enough moisture has been removed. A broken curd should be firm throughout and the curds should have a moderate resistance when pressed between the fingers.

When this point is reached, the curds can be allowed to settle under the whey then remove 50% of the whey to just above the curd level. The whey removal will slow the bacteria activity by removing a good portion of it's food source (lactose in whey).

This would be a good time to make sure the draining cloth and colander have been sanitized and ready for the curd transfer after the next step.

- Wash Curds

This next step is specific to the Jack style cheese and involves washing the curds with cool water (60F). This will result in a higher moisture curd as the cool water begins to migrate into the curd. At the same time this will cool the cheese and further reduce the activity of the bacteria due to the cooling cheese mass.

Add enough of the 60°F water (about 3-4 quarts) to cool the curds to 86°F, then continue to stir the curds over the next 15 minutes. This should have taken about 4.5 hours up to this point and the curds should be ready to transfer.

- Drain Curds

This would be a good time to weigh out the salt because the salt will be added to the curds before molding. I find the curd weight to be about 6.25 lbs and I use about 2.5% salt (2.5 ozs). This tends to provide about 1.7-1/9% salt in the final cheese, considering the brine lost in whey run-off during pressing.

The whey can now be removed again down to the curd level and the dry curds can be transferred to a colander lined with butter muslin. They should be allowed to drain for 10-20 minutes and a gentle stirring will make sure that the whey drains off.

- Salt Curds

The salt can now be added to the drained curd in 2 separate additions, while stirring the curds well for salt distribution and to encourage the final whey drainage. Leave about 10 minutes between additions to allow the salt to dissolve and be absorbed by the curd.

- Form the Cheese

The next step begins the curd consolidation and shaping of the final form (I just think this is such an interesting and simple way to form a cheese). It's only drawback is the limited weight that the cloth will take, but this is the way it has been made since the 'get-go' and I do love a challenge.

Begin by gathering the four corners of the cloth and pulling them together to enclose the curd mass. You want to have a big enough cloth so that there are no gaps below the knot. Next the curd mass is gently formed into a round ball while pulling the loose ends of cloth up through your grip as the curd begins to consolidate into it's final form. This final form is accomplished with the help of a firmer hand pressure and in some cases a bit of body weight on the ball, along with a lot of rolling back and forth on a smooth surface. A large tray will be useful for this because some whey is still running off during the process.

- Pressing

Once the curd is formed into a nice tight round ball, the cloth should be tied off tight and as close to the curd mass as possible. The next step is to place the ball with the knot upwards on a hard board and spread the cloth as evenly as possible around the surface.

Following this, another board is placed on top.

Now for the challenge of keeping a board and weight level on top of a round ball. I will leave you to your own inventive ways for this, but what I have done here is to use the edge of my draining sink as a stable surface to keep a third board anchored and then with spacers between the top press board and the third board, I have a rather stable and level platform for my weights. The photos should make this pretty clear. As the weight compresses the curd, more spacers were added to keep the top board level to prevent a lop-sided cheese.

This pressing is much more simplified when done in a larger production because they have many of these being pressed under a much larger board. I believe they use large plastic buckets of water for the weight as well. For pressing weight you should begin very light and slowly increase the weight to a moderate level:

- 2 hours at 25 lbs.
- 8-12 hours at 50 lbs

- Pressing (cont.)

The next morning, the cheese should be well formed and fully consolidated. If it is not, then a longer pressing with increased weight should be done until you see a fully consolidated cheese. The top of the cheese will show the unique pattern of the cloth and a small 'belly button' where the cloth was tied, but the bottom and sides should show a nice smooth surface.

Allow the new cheese to dry at room temp for 5-10 days until the surface seems dry to the touch. Avoid too dry a space to prevent any cracking or curd separation. It should be turned daily and any mold that appears should be rubbed off with a medium textured cloth or brush as shown above. At the end of this drying time the surface will have begun to dry more and be ready for it's final surface rub.

- Create & Apply Surface Rub

Here is where the fun begins. The dark rub will create a surface that is less attractive to molds and be easier to keep clean. I also think that it adds a bit of aroma and flavor to the cheese.

Prepare the rub:

- 1tsp espresso beans
- 2 tbs cocoa nibs
- 1.5 tsp black pepper
- 3-3.5 tbs olive oil

Above, shows a collection of cocoa nibs (raw unsweetened), dark espresso beans, and black pepper, all needing to be ground fine before adding to the oil. Begin with the cheese that has been drying for a few days in the aging space and has been cleaned of any mold that developed during that time.

Next, we gather our ingredients for the rub as shown above. It is best to reduce them to a very fine powder to make the smoothest paste for application. I have found it best to make this a day before the application because the powder takes some time to absorb the oil. The paste needs to be mixed very well and you may find that more oil is needed as the ingredients absorb the oil.

Now, it's time to return to our younger side to get our hands in the mud and rub it all over the surface. Make sure you rub it into all of the cracks and crevices.

- Re-Apply Surface Rub

Wait 2 or 3 days and repeat the rub. Two to three applications should be sufficient to protect the surface. If it does seem to dry out, you can rub the surface with just a little oil again. The oil is what keeps the mold from getting serious about attaching to the surface.

Aging should then continue as before with 52-56F and 80-85% moisture, turning and wiping any surface mold as it develops. The amount of time you age should be at least 6-9 months, but better if you can hold out and age it for a year and longer.

Simple Farm Cheese

This simple farm cheese can come together quickly. It tastes mild and sweet, and doesn't require rennet, making an excellent cheese for beginners.

- Cook Time: 1 hr 20 mins
- Total Time: 2 hrs 20 mins

Ingredients:

- 1 gallon whole milk not ultrapasteurized
- ½ cup white vinegar
- 2 teaspoons finely ground real salt

Instructions:

- Line a colander with a double layer of cheesecloth or a single layer of butter muslin (find it here).
- Pour the milk into a large, heavy-bottomed kettle, and bring it to a boil over medium heat. Stir it frequently to keep the milk from scorching. When it comes to a boil, immediately reduce the heat to low, and stir in the vinegar.
- The milk should immediately separate into curds and whey. If it does not separate, add a bit more vinegar one tablespoon at a time until you see the milk solids coagulate into curds swimming within the thin greenish blue whey.

- Pour the curds and whey into the lined colander. Rinse them gently with cool water, and sprinkle the curds with salt. Tie up the cheesecloth, and press it a bit with your hands to remove excess whey. Let the cheesecloth hang for 1 to 2 hours, then open it up and chop it coarsely. Store in the fridge for up to a week.

Notes:

You may set the lined colander over a bucket or crock to catch they whey rather than discarding it; however, keep in mind that it is not a cultured food, and if you are accustomed to using whey as a starter culture for fermented vegetables, it will not work as it doesn't contain live active bacteria. It can, however, be reserved for feeding pigs and chickens, or for soaking grains and flour.

Stirred-Curd Cheddar

Stirred-curd cheddar, similar to farmhouse cheddar, could also be called "shortcut cheddar," for it is a faster and easier way to make this popular cheese. Traditional cheddars take longer and require more attention to detail, while this type of cheddar is good for both beginning cheesemakers and those with less time to devote to cheesemaking.

Ingredients:

- 2 gallons whole milk
- 1 packet direct-set mesophilic culture
- 1/2 tsp. liquid rennet diluted in 1/4 cup water
- 2 Tbsp. cheese salt

You can also color this cheese, if you wish. If you are going to do this, you can have 4 drops of cheese coloring diluted in 1/4 cup water ready to go.

Instructions:

- Heat the milk to 90°F. Add the starter and mix it in using an up-and-down motion for 1 minute. Cover milk and leave it to ripen for 45 minutes.
- Mix in the coloring, if you are using it, and stir it in using an up-and-down motion.

- Check to make sure the milk is still 90°F. If it isn't, bring the temperature back up. Add the rennet and stir in using the same up-and-down gentle motions for 1 minute. If you are using farm-fresh cow milk, top-stir for 2 more minutes. Cover your milk and allow it to set at 90°F for 45 more minutes, making sure you keep a steady 90°F temperature.

- Once you have a clean break, cut the curd into 1/4-inch cubes.

- Allow the curds to set for 15 minutes, then heat them to 100°F, bringing the temperature up by a maximum of 2°F every 5 minutes. Stir frequently to keep the curds from sticking together (matting). Once the curds reach 100°F, maintain the temperature for 30 more minutes, and keep stirring periodically but not continually. After the last 30 minutes is up, cover the curds and whey and let them rest for 5 minutes.

- Drain off the whey and pour the curds into a colander suspended over a large bowl. Drain them for several minutes, then pour the curds back into the pot and stir them with your fingers. Don't allow your curds to drain in the colander for too long, or they will begin to mat. If some have matted by the time you have dumped them back into the pot, very gently break them up with your fingers.

- Add the salt to the curds in the pot and mix it in well. Try not to squeeze the curds.

- Keep the curds in the pot at 100°F for 1 hour, stirring them with your fingers every now and again to keep them from matting. (You can fill a sink or a large bowl with water and set your pot into it, and keep the surrounding water at 100°F by taking out some water when the temperature begins to drop and adding heated water until it reaches the proper temperature again.)

- Scoop the curds into a 2-pound cheese press lined with cheesecloth. Press at 15 pounds of pressure for 2 minutes.

- Remove the cheese from the press, peel off the cheesecloth, flip the cheese, re-dress it, and put it back into the press at 30 pounds of pressure for 10 minutes.

- Remove, undress, flip, and re-dress the cheese. Place it back into the press at 40 pounds of pressure for 2 hours.

- Remove, undress, flip, and re-dress the cheese. Place it back into the press at 50 pounds of pressure for 24 hours.

- Remove the finished cheese from the press. Peel away the cheesecloth and dry the cheese on a drying mat at room temperature away from drafts for 3 to 5 days or until the rind is dry to the touch. Flip it about 5 times a day during the drying process. After it has dried, wax it and age it at 45° to 50°F for 2 to 5 months.

Mascarpone Cheese

Mascarpone is a light and fluffy soft cheese that is traditionally used to make tiramisù and cannoli. Alternatively, mascarpone is delicious mounded in a bowl and topped with fresh fruit.

- Prep Time: 20 Minutes
- Cook Time: 2 Hours, 25 Minutes
- Total Time: 2 Hours, 45 Minutes
- Yield : Makes About 1 Quart.

Ingredients:

- 1 quart cream or half-and-half
- ¼ tsp. tartaric acid or 2 tablespoons lemon juice
- Thermometer
- Butter muslin or tight-weave cloth

Instructions:

- In a double boiler, gently heat cream to 190°F. Use a thermometer to avoid overheating.
- While cream is heating, dissolve tartaric acid in 2 Tbsp. of water.
- Once the cream has reached 190°F, remove from heat and add the tartaric acid solution. Whisk thoroughly into the cream for 30 seconds.
- Allow the cream mixture to sit for 5 minutes, stirring occasionally. The cream will thicken to a consistency similar to farina and should coat the back of the spoon.
- Place a colander in a bowl and line the colander with sterile butter muslin or a sterile tea towel. Pour the coagulated cream into the cloth and let the whey drain for 1 to 2 hours or until the desired consistency is achieved.
- Spoon the mascarpone into a storage container and place in the refrigerator to chill. As it chills it will continue to thicken a bit. While mascarpone should be consumed within a day or two for optimal flavor, it can be stored in the refrigerator for up to a week.

Conclusion.

Farm stead cheese are easy to make if necessary instructions are thoroughy followed,